The Adventures of
"Smart Bart"

The Adventures of "Smart Bart"
The Guide Dog
SUMMER VACATION

J. Patricia Cowan

Illustrated by
Nicholas A. Welmaker

iUniverse, Inc.
New York Lincoln Shanghai

The Adventures of "Smart Bart"
The Guide Dog

iUniverse books may be ordered through booksellers or by contacting:

iUniverse
2021 Pine Lake Road, Suite 100
Lincoln, NE 68512
www.iuniverse.com
1-800-Authors (1-800-288-4677)

ISBN-13: 978-0-595-33410-0 (pbk)
ISBN-13: 978-0-595-66907-3 (cloth)
ISBN-13: 978-0-595-78207-9 (ebk)
ISBN-10: 0-595-33410-5 (pbk)
ISBN-10: 0-595-66907-7 (cloth)
ISBN-10: 0-595-78207-8 (ebk)

Printed in the United States of America

✟

In Loving Memory of

Bonnie Shirley Burnett

And

Ernie Cody

Two very dear and precious friends

Contents

From the Author's Heart

Dear Reader,

Thank you for choosing the <u>Adventures of Smart Bart</u>, the Guide Dog. This delightful adventure is a true story. Readers from eight to eighty will find this little book filled with moments of refreshing joy. As you read this book, you will discover relaxing moments, teaching moments, and adventurous moments filled with suspense. Allow your thoughts to be transformed to life lived on the mountain. Books are for lingering; cherish the images you will find dancing in your own imagination.

Why would I encourage you to do this? For many years, I took these simple pleasures for granted and failed to appreciate the little things in life. It was only after I lost my eyesight that I realized what is truly important in this world. It is often through adversity that we reach for strength greater than our own. In renewing my faith in God, I found that all things were possible through Him. God allowed me to focus on the things He would have me to see—through the eyes of my gentle guide dog.

To help young readers understand words they may not be familiar with, you will find a glossary located in the back of this book. For an adult reading to a child, this is a perfect opportunity to review the unfamiliar word and discuss it with the child. For the more mature reader, I hope you will find it enjoyable to refresh your own memory.

Throughout each chapter, there is a little "lesson of life" that I have learned through my own walk of faith. I share a few of these lessons with you. Since losing my eyesight, I now "walk by faith, not by sight" and see more with my heart than I ever saw with my eyes.

Author, Pat Cowan

Dank

Acknowledgements

To my devoted husband, his love has sustained me, his faith has never faltered.

To my friends who gave me courage, you may find yourself in this little story.

To Bonnie, thank you for your everlasting friendship and strength.

❧❦

Also, to Southeastern Guide Dogs for selecting my first guide dog, "Bart," the perfect match for me, my exceptional guide dog—a dear companion, and a cherished friend. He is more than I ever hoped for, more than words could ever express. To Southeastern Guide Dogs for providing a life long commitment to our success as a team for Bart's working life.

To Katherine Ulrich, my first Southeastern Instructor in 1992 whose professionalism and vast training knowledge surpassed her young years. Her passion for excellence only ignited my own passion to overcome whatever obstacles came my way.

enorm   *über treffen*   *to i, ansunden*

To Rick Holden, Southeastern's Director of Training, a man of compassion and integrity, who challenges his instructors to never settle for "less than the best" for the students and the dogs.

aufordern

To Linda Sylvester for providing technical assistance and encouragement to bring this book to life.

There have been many encouragers in my life, more than I could possibly list on one page. Since losing my eyesight in 1991 the individuals listed above have made a significant positive difference in my life. Thank you all for making my life full and rewarding.

Thank you for touching my life in so many ways.

J. Patricia Cowan

Note:

A portion of the proceeds from the sale of this book will go to Southeastern Guide Dogs, Inc. to further their Mission of helping blind and visually impaired individuals.

1

I have been awake for a while, but Miss Pat is a sleepyhead this morning and does not want to get up. As I lean against the side of the bed, her hand automatically slides down to pet my head. I nuzzle her fingers and lick her hand. Wake up! Wake up! I want to say. I need to go out, and I am very hungry! Good, I finally have her attention! She slips out of bed rubbing the sleep from her eyes as she changes from her pajamas into her shorts and tee shirt. She does not need to turn on the lights. Walking around in the dark is no problem for her. It is very early and everyone in the neighborhood is still sleeping.

My name is "Smart Bart." Anyway, that is what Miss Pat has always called me. I'm her working guide dog, a *Labrador*. Miss Pat and I have been together a little over a year. A very special school in Florida, Southeastern Guide Dogs, Inc., matched me to Miss Pat. I was born and raised with a special purpose for my life and I have been waiting for the time that I would meet my new master.

In a soft voice she tells me, "your coat is as soft as black velvet," as she stoops down to rub my head again. My coat is shiny, and very black. Miss Pat reaches for my red collar on her bedside table. We must put it on before going outside. She places it there each night because she says it jiggles and makes too much noise with my *identification* tags attached. The tags are important. I have to wear them during the day, but not at night when she puts me to bed.

Long before I knew Miss Pat, her eyes became very sick. They began to grow dim and then dimmer until finally one day she could not see faces anymore. Her eye doctor said she was losing her eyesight. She had heard how guide dogs assisted visually *impaired* and blind people and decided a guide dog, just like me, would be a great help to her. This is what I was born to do; what I was trained for. That was the beginning for us.

Enough about that for now, I will be telling you more about my training and guide dog school later. Let's get going on our walk. She is all ready, and so am I. I know where the leash is since she always keeps it on a hook right by the back door. There, she has the leash. Hurry, Miss Pat, I really have to go out! Whew, that is a relief. I really had to go, if you know what I mean!

Back in the house, she takes my harness off the hook, near where my leash hangs. We cannot take our walk in the neighborhood until I have my harness on. Miss Pat ties a brightly colored scarf around my neck, and then puts my harness on me. This morning my scarf is bright red. Everyone says I am so handsome. Yes, I guess I am. She has told me it is important for me to look my best. Wait, do you know what a harness is? If not, I will tell you.

A harness is very necessary piece of equipment for a guide dog. It is handmade of smooth brown leather, and it fits snugly around my chest and my tummy. It is very comfortable. My harness is designed with a long handle on the top, which Miss Pat holds as we walk. By holding the handle of the harness, she can feel my body move as I slow down or stop.

My harness has the name of my school on the top of it, Southeastern Guide Dogs, Inc. That is where I received my training to become a professional guide dog.

Some guide dogs have a little sign on their harness that says, "Please don't pet me, I am a working guide dog." That is true, but I do not have that sign on my harness because Miss Pat prefers to talk to people if they show an interest in me. She takes time to chat a moment with them about me and the work I do, answering all their questions. She says they learn more this way. However, Miss Pat does tell people not to pet me while I am working, but only because it is *distracting* and she knows I need to keep my attention on her. There can be no playing around while on duty! That is her rule.

Our morning walks are my most favorite time of day. Miss Pat talks to me all the while we walk. This morning she seems happier than usual! She is telling me that we have many errands to do today so we must hurry with our walk. We do not usually hurry on our morning walks. I wonder, why today. What we will be doing? She knows morning time is a very special time for me.

Just the two of us walking and talking, only she does all the talking. As we walk, I will be watching for any holes or big cracks in the sidewalk and for the curbs at the street, so she will not trip or stumble. When I see something in our path that might cause her to trip or stumble, I slow down letting her know we need to proceed slowly.

It is still very dark out this morning, with only the occasional driver going to work before dawn. "Plop! Plop!" Yes, I hear it too, Miss Pat. That is the sound of the newspaperman throwing the morning papers on the driveways. "Plop! Plop!" We hear that sound every morning, every day. He is very *faithful* doing his job, just like me, very faithful.

As I focus on the sidewalk ahead—I see something! Yes, that's an obstacle all right! She reacts automatically to my pace and proceeds with caution, now aware that there may be something in our path. It is a garbage can, turned over on the sidewalk. Today must be Tuesday—trash pickup day. There are always things to watch for on that day! As we get closer to the *obstacle,* I begin to walk even slower and she slows *instinctively.* I stop, she stops. She puts her right foot out to feel what is in our path. She knows now what it is. She says "Good Boy, Bart," pleased that I kept her from bumping into the messy trashcan. She tells me it is "O.K." and gives me the guide dog *command* "around." I proceed to lead her around and to the edge of the walk, passing safely, and then back on the sidewalk. She tells me "Good job." We are on our way again.

Trashcans can be a problem in our path, but curbs are especially important for me to watch for also. She tells me to "find the curb!" This is another guide dog command. Commands are instructions she uses to help me make the right decisions. She does not want to trip on the curb, but more importantly, she will not step out into the street before knowing when it is safe to cross.

I know you always stop at the street corner and look both ways for traffic before proceeding to cross, just like I do. Remember, never, ever run into the street! Some dogs might do this, but I never would! It is not a safe thing to do for any of us—pets, dogs, or people.

2

I learned many, many guide dog commands when trained at my special school. Things like: find the steps, find the curb, find the walk, find the elevator, find the trash can, find the steps, go around, over right, and over left. When I graduated from school, I knew about forty different commands. Now I know many more than that! Miss Pat thought it was important for me to learn other commands that she knew we would need. We had to learn all the commands and how to use them before we could graduate. But, we did it—we know them all! We are always together and she keeps me very busy. Almost any place she wants to go, I go. I help her cross the streets and guide her as she visits the grocery store, shops in the mall, and goes to the hairdresser. Probably the hardest part of my job is the shopping mall and the airports! Most people forget to look where they are going because they are in such a big hurry. This makes my job difficult, but not impossible. Besides, *impossible* for us is only temporary!

I knew from the time I was a puppy I had a special purpose in life. I would be trained to assist a person who could not see, I would be their eyes. I would need to learn many things as I grew. First, I would need to obey, then to be sure of my surroundings, and of course, to love *unconditionally*.

I know so much more now about traveling in all different places. I tried my very best while I was in guide dog training to learn as much as possible in those two years. Your schoolwork is a lot like my training. It is teaching you things you will need to know for the world we live in. Sometimes the lessons are difficult, sometimes they are fun, but always, they are necessary to prepare us for our future.

It seems like I waited a long time to meet the person I would guide. There will be many things Miss Pat and I will experience for the first time together. Our *adventure* is just beginning.

It seems such a long time since I left my guide dog school. Time has had no meaning to me since meeting Miss Pat. Those were very tiring days as we went through our training together. Then, almost a month later, it was graduation day!

I remember the day of our graduation very well. Pop came to see us walk proudly across the campus and toward the Director of Training to accept our certificate. "Pop" is Miss Pat's husband. Miss Pat and I had passed all the training tests, and finally one day the Training Instructors said, "you two are a real team, you are ready for graduation." We had done it! We were so proud. That is when our life together really began. One day you will graduate from your school too. This will be a very special day for you, just as it was for Miss Pat and me.

We are always learning. What is a problem today is not a problem tomorrow, because we learn how to find a *solution* for it. Learning a little something everyday helps us to grow stronger and more confident in what we do. For me, learning is fun. I make it a game. I call the game, "What I will learn new today."

Pop is a very patient, very kind man. Pop loved me from the first day Miss Pat brought me home. He knew I was a specially trained dog to help Miss Pat and assist with her *mobility*. Pop could see instantly how much I already loved her. I think he could see it in my eyes. My eyes are deep chocolate brown with little glints of gold. I have heard Miss Pat say, "she can see with her heart." I don't really understand what that means, but she seems to understand things she cannot see. She is always saying, "God is so good."

As we finish our morning walk and turn back into our walkway, she tells me, "Smart Bart, Pop will be driving us today." I am glad we will be with Pop today because he has been very busy lately. Sometimes when Pop is at work, we have friends who pick us up in their car to take us places, or we may schedule a ride on one of the city's Handi-busses. The Handi-bus is a specially equipped bus we use which provides transportation for people with special needs. The bus has wheelchair ramps, lifts, and handrails to assist people getting on and off the bus. The drivers are very polite and helpful. It is very convenient to have this type of *transportation* in our city.

Miss Pat tells me all the plans for the day. Her plans are always my plans. Wherever she goes, I go. That is what guide dogs do so that we are always together. When she talks to me, sometimes she tells me God has a plan for her too. What a great job I have. We are always moving forward with determination and *confidence*. For a dog, that's not bad!

As we are walking, Miss Pat has her morning *conversation* with God. I think He is her best friend. I often hear her praying aloud as we walk. She asks God to lead us both this day, and keep us safe. She prays for all our friends and those who may be sick or lonely. Miss Pat never seems to get lonely, because she says God has promised her that He will never leave her, nor forsake her. That's a promise! God never breaks a promise. Have you ever made a promise? Do you always keep your promises?

Life for me is so simple, but it seems life for big people is not so simple. People sometimes have *complicated* lives, so much to do, so much to think about, so many places to go. Speaking of going, I better get ready for our errands, since she said we have so many today.

3

Each day we have our morning routine. It may be a little different from yours. First, we go for our two-mile walk and then we go back home for my breakfast. It is the same thing everyday—but always good! I then get my breakfast of dry dog food and fresh water. Miss Pat eats only "people" food. Guide dogs are not allowed people food. She usually eats the same thing everyday too: cereal, fruit, and hot tea. Sometimes she makes hot oatmeal. It does not look appetizing to me, but she seems to like it very much. I guess that is what she ate when she was a little puppy—oops, I mean a baby. People are not puppies when they are born, only dogs like me are puppies when we are born!

After we have filled our tummies, she clears away the dirty dishes and washes my bowl, refilling it with cool water. Now it is time for more morning routine stuff. She goes to brush her teeth and then when she is finished, it's my turn. Miss Pat brushes my teeth with my own special toothbrush. She cleans my long floppy ears, inside and out with a soft cotton ball. It tickles, but I stay still. I love the gentle way she helps me with things I could not do for myself. I do things for her that she cannot do for herself. Remember, that's my job. Can you name some of the things I do in my job for Miss Pat? Do remember any of the guide dog commands I told you about earlier?

Later, we sit outside on the *lanai* and she brushes my fur. This is my most favorite part of my grooming time. Oh—it feels so good! She doesn't give me a bath everyday. A bath everyday is only for people. Remember, I am a big black Labrador. Did you know Labradors love the water? I wish I could have a bath everyday. I would play in the water and splash. No wait, that would not be a good thing to do because it would get Miss Pat all wet. When she is giving me my bath, she tells me "No shake." After my bath is finished, she lets me shake, shake, shake! I like the feel of my favorite big fluffy towel as she dries my coat. She would let me splash all I wanted if we were at the beach!

Once we are finished with my grooming, we do our homework. We have homework everyday. Just like you, rain or shine, our homework must be done except for Saturdays and Sundays. I bet you just love the weekend. I know I do! I do not have homework on weekends! However, my homework is a bit different from yours. I do not read books, so I must pay very close attention and listen carefully to each instruction. Remember, instructions given to me by Miss Pat are commands. It is very important that I understand and obey. My homework consists of "daily obedience." We do our obedience for twenty minutes each morning and night. It is what guide dogs are supposed to do. We must remember all the things that we are taught.

My obedience is a little boring at times and Miss Pat seems to sense this, so she makes it fun by having me do "doggie *aerobics*." Miss Pat will say, "sit," then "down," then "sit," then "down." Whew! After about four or five of those exercises, I am ready for a short rest. She knows these exercises keep me strong and fit. It is a good workout, and fun. Finally, we are finished with obedience for this morning. She brushes me one more time to make sure my coat is all shiny and smooth. I look great! As she gets up, putting my brushes away neatly, she says, "Smart Bart," come. I must hurry with my shower!" After finishing with her shower, we get ready for the many errands we have to do.

Wait! Why is she getting our suitcases from the closet?

4

I hear the garage door opening. It must be Pop. Yes, it is Pop. He has come home to drive us to do the special shopping Miss Pat said we had to do today. She hurries to meet him and seems excited about the plans for the day. What could we be doing? She hasn't told me yet! By now, I usually know where we will be going and who will be picking us up to drive us. Today seems very different to me! I watch as she puts my harness in the back seat and says, "come, 'Smart Bart', and load up!" Do you remember what my "harness" is for and why it is used?

Pop holds the car door open for me. I jump up in the back seat of the car and listen intently as they talk excitedly about all the shopping errands. "We will need a sweater, some hiking boots, some candles, and a canteen," she tells Pop. He agrees as he carefully pulls out into traffic. Right now, he is in charge, not me. I cannot drive a car—dogs don't drive! That would look silly. I do not have my harness on either, but when we stop to go into the store, she will put it on me. When I have my harness on, it is work time. For me, it is no time to be goofing off. If you are at the mall or store and see a guide dog like me working, remember not to "pet" the dog, because it is working.

As I listen, I hear Miss Pat and Pop talking about going away for a whole month! Yes, yes, now I understand, we are going on vacation! They are talking about the mountains in North Carolina. Wow! That sounds terrific! This will be my first time in the mountains. It will be very different from Florida.

Of course Miss Pat and Pop always take me on our family trips, because guide dogs are allowed to go on airplanes, trains, buses, and even stay in the motel and hotel rooms. We will be together on the trip. She would never leave me, nor would I leave her. She needs me, and I need her, she loves me, and I love her. She told me once how much God loves all His children. She must feel very safe knowing God is always near. I'm glad she also feels safe with me. I will do my very best to take care of her.

The first time we met, she was not all sure of herself, nor had she had time to learn to trust me. During our time at guide dog school together, she learned that I had all the necessary training to accomplish my job well. She asked God to give her back her confidence, and He did. I will help with that too over the coming years.

5

When we go on trips, I still have to "work" guiding Miss Pat, because she cannot see as well as me. It is my job to help her. When she is ready to leave, she will say, "Come 'Smart Bart', let's go to work." To me, my work is always fun, just one more adventure. I'm sure I will love this trip to the mountains. Mountains are another one of the beautiful places God created. Everything He created is lovely in His eyes. Sometimes I wish people could see through His eyes. Then they would know that He beautifully and wonderfully makes everything.

In one of the first stories in the Bible, you can read all about how God created the whole universe and the world we live in. He made everything, the oceans, the rivers, the flowers, the trees, the insects, the animals, the weeds and the bees, and much, much, more. In the beginning, there was so much to create—how *awesome*!

God made the tall swaying palm trees and lovely gulf beaches in Florida, where we live. He even made the mosquitoes and fleas! I may want to ask Him someday, why He made fleas. He even made the manatees that live in the warm gulf waters. Manatees are gentle sea cows, but they do not look like any cow I ever saw. God created all the sea creatures, including the whales from the deep cooler waters.

I've heard about mountains, but have never seen any. I know they are part of God's creations so they must be a very special. Miss Pat told me the land is very high. Up and down, up and down. The land has many twisting, winding narrow roads. Some mountains have huge granite rocks. Between the mountains are the lush green valleys. A good place to run and romp I think.

Where we live, the land is flat. We live on the west coast of Florida, near the *Gulf* of Mexico. The beaches are made of soft white sand. The gulf waters are warm and deep blue-green. Beaches and mountains—both are beautiful, in their own special ways. Just the way God made us different from each other, but very special in our own way, some tall, some short, some light, some dark. There are so many people and animals all living together in this big old world.

Some people live in the mountains or the deep valleys all year. Some live in the big cities, or way out in the Western states. Some live up North, where the winters are cold with snow. Some people live in the very dry desert regions, or the jungles of faraway lands. God's earth and universe is so big, I cannot even imagine it all. Can you name some other different places you have been, or where other people live? I think you can. You are very smart!

On some of our evening walks, we talk about the big *universe*, the stars, and the big bright moon. Miss Pat told me that at night, everyone all over the world could see these same stars and moon. It makes me feel very small when I think of how big and magnificent the universe is.

I often wonder—how do the stars stay up in the sky and not fall down? When does the moon sleep? For all this to work properly and perfectly I know God is in control. He takes care of everything, even when I don't understand the things I see or hear.

Miss Pat says, "God loves us all. He only wants what is best for us." We often make mistakes, but no matter what, God still loves us! That's called "unconditional love." Do you know what *unconditional* means?

I've been daydreaming as we waited for Pop to fill up the car with gas for the errands. We still have all that shopping to do. I'm ready, let's get going!

Our shopping for the trip is finally finished. "Honk! Honk!" There's Pop, he's right by the curb. "Let's hurry" Miss Pat commands as she points forward with her hand.

It is summertime, so today it has been very hot. Miss Pat sometimes asks Pop to take us up to the front door of the store so I don't have to walk on the hot parking lot pavement. Once she stopped and took off her shoe as we came out of the store. At first, I did not know why she would do that. Then I saw her put her barefoot down on the pavement to see if it was too hot. "Ouch!" she said. "Pop, would you please go get the car. This will be much too hot for Smart Bart. Thank you dear," she said as he willing agreed to go get the car. Pop told us to wait inside the store out of the heat until he returned with the car.

I am tired after we walked through so many stores finding all the things on Miss Pat's list. My paws are ready for the soft cool carpet of our house. Oh, that feels so good, yes, now I can rest for a while. Miss Pat kicks off her shoes and wiggles her toes in the carpet as well. We all rest after the big shopping trip.

Pop has begun loading the car with everything we will need for our trip. Let's see, did Pop forget anything? My food, my dog dish, my toys, my toothbrush, my blanket, my vitamins, my hairbrush—nope, that's it! We have everything. Well maybe not everything, I guess they need their people stuff too! I should not be only thinking of myself. After all, this is a family trip.

There are many things to do. First, Pop needed to take the car to the service shop to be sure it is in good working order. Now that has been done, Miss Pat reminds Pop to check over their list of things to do before leaving the house. "Let's see," he says, "the newspaper has been stopped, the mail will be held by the post office, and the patio furniture has all been stored *securely* in the garage." Pop has taken care of everything.

We have a big blue ice chest filled with ice and cool drinks for the trip. I saw Miss Pat put in some grapes, an apple and several oranges as well. The fruit smells great, I wish she would give me a bite before we leave. I guess not right now, they will make a great snack later. We all settle back to enjoy the trip. As Pop pulls out of the driveway, he puts a map in the front seat of the car. Miss Pat laughs and says, "you don't expect me to read that for you, do you?" He laughs. "No, dear, I know how to get to North Carolina, it's just in case I need it." We are on our way! I'm so excited thinking about our first summer adventure. I will try to be patient, after all this is my first long road trip. I love being in the car with Pop and Miss Pat. I listen quietly as they discuss what we will be doing and what friends we will visit.

6

We will have to travel a very long time to get to the mountains—maybe two days. I don't mind because we will be stopping at rest areas often for a break. Guide dogs are allowed in the Rest Areas and Welcome Stations along the highway. Besides, Pop will need to get out of the car to stretch his legs since he is the only one driving. Miss Pat is telling Pop she is thirsty and needs a break soon.

Pop spots a rest area just ahead. He carefully pulls off the interstate highway and drives to the area where cars are suppose to park. Trucks have to park in another area made just for them. I'm panting heavily and Miss Pat knows I am thirsty. She opens the cooler and pours some fresh water into my bowl. She is ready to get out of the car too. I will run and play a few minutes with Miss Pat then I will need to go "busy-busy"(that means I have to go poop and pee-pee). It's not only me, we will all need go to the bathroom.

Miss Pat puts on my harness and I jump out of the car. I am so glad to stretch my legs. First I need to help Miss Pat find the ladies bathroom, a few people stare as she quietly gives me the command, "Bart, find the ladies room." I quickly take her into the correct door marked "Women." No, I don't know how to read, I just learned how to find the ladies room when we travel on business. After we come out, I need to go "busy-busy" so she digs into her purse and finds a plastic bag. O.K., she has it, we're off to the pet walking area.

My potty area is outside on the grass. She will clean up after me with the "busy bag." Everyone should pick up after his or her dog has gone "busy." It is the polite thing to do.

People know that pets are not allowed in the public bathrooms, but I am not a "pet." I am a Service Animal. Service Animals are allowed in all public places. There are signs at the highway rest areas that read, "Dog Guides and Service Animals Welcome." That's so cool. They say we are "welcome." I like that. Service Dogs help people who may need special *assistance*. Ask your mom or dad to look for a sign that reads, "Dog Guides and Service Animals Welcome" the next time you are on a long trip. I have learned so much since becoming a guide dog. I guess I am "Smart Bart" all right!

Pop is calling us: "Pat, Bart—we need to get going. We still have long way to go." We hurry back to the car, feeling relaxed and refreshed after the break from riding. My harness is removed, and I jump up in the back seat. I have the back seat of the car all to myself. Feeling much better, I'm ready for a nice nap. It is very cozy back here with my soft blanket. I have a small blue pillow and my favorite toy.

I have only been sleeping for a short while when I hear the noise! What is that? It sounds like someone is throwing rocks on our car. Bang, thump, ping—what is that? I sit up—and Miss Pat immediately says, "Bart—down, and stay!"

7

As I peer out the back window, I realize a thunderstorm has come up and it is raining very hard! Pop is watching the road carefully and going much slower than before. I hear him tell Miss Pat, "Honey, if this keeps up, we will need to stop early at a motel for the night. This is quite a storm, and many of the cars are pulling off the road because they can't see well enough to drive." Miss Pat listens carefully as she notices concern in his voice. She calmly says, "That sounds like a good idea, Honey. We can get a fresh start again in the morning. You have been driving over seven hours today, anyway. The break will make the rest of the trip seem short." Pop agrees. He begins to watch for an exit off the interstate with a nice motel where we will spend the night.

The weather outside may be all wet and stormy, but it has not dampened our spirits at all. Pop begins to slow down when he sees a sign for the next exit. He says, "There's a good motel ahead. It will be a comfortable place for us to stay this evening." He carefully leaves the highway and looks for the motel. "Yes, there it is" he says. Pop turns our car into the driveway leading to the motel. Under the *portico* of the motel, it is nice and dry. Pop said to us, "Would you two like to get out while I get us checked in?" Yes, a stretch is what we both need! After Miss Pat slips her shoes back on, she reaches behind her seat to get my harness. Pop gets out of the car and goes around the car to open the car door for her. I stand ready to hop out and have my harness put on.

It is still raining heavily and the wind is blowing hard. It has gotten very dark outside. We all hurry inside the motel. Miss Pat tells me, "Smart Bart, find a seat." Yes, there is a nice comfortable chair where we can wait as Pop checks us in.

"Good afternoon" Pop says to the motel registration clerk. "My wife and I need a room for the evening, please. By the way, as you can see, we are traveling with my wife's guide dog."

The young man behind the desk seems pleasant, but looks at Pop strangely. He says, "Sir, we have a *policy,* dogs are not allowed in the rooms of our motel. However, we do have a nice pet kennel outside. It is dry and comfortable." Pop says with assuredness, but kindness in his voice, "Thank you, but no, that will not be acceptable. You see, my wife's black Lab is not a pet, he is a working guide dog. Guide dogs are allowed in all public *accommodations*." The man appears embarrassed as he says, "Sir, that is our policy and I can't make any exceptions."

Pop politely asks to see the manager of the motel. The reservation clerk makes a few calls and shortly a young woman appears behind the desk. "May I be of some assistance here," she asks. "Yes. I would like a room for my wife, her guide dog and myself for the evening please," Pop says. The reservations clerk interrupts and says, "I told the gentleman we do not accept dogs in the room," eager to let his employer know he was only doing his job. The motel manager seems a little annoyed, but smiles to her employee as she says, "The policy does not include guide dogs." Looking back at Pop she says, "Sir, we will be happy to assist you with your registration." So—she was aware of the rules of traveling with a working guide dog, however, apparently she had forgotten to convey that information to this new employee. She says she will certainly find a comfortable room for us on the ground level floor.

Finally, Pop walks over to where we are waiting patiently. Miss Pat says, "What took you so long honey?" She had heard the conversation take place. However, she was not aware of what was being said because she was listening to the TV weather report in the lobby area.

He tells her what had happened at the desk, but states everything is fine now. He said, "The manager apologized for the delay in checking in and wishes us a pleasant evening." Miss Pat and Pop continue to talk a few minutes about what to take out of the car for the evening. He tells her he needs to move our car. She replies O.K., "Smart Bart and I will remain here until you get back so we don't get wet. It is still raining outside." Pop drives around to find our room. Once the car is parked, he returns to the lobby from the inside hallway and walks with us to our room. It is a nice room with a view of the courtyard.

After we are settled in our room Miss Pat asks Pop, "Do you think there is anything I can explain to the management staff here to help them understand the rules of traveling with a guide dog?" "No, not this time," says Pop. "The manager is well aware. It appears to just be a lack of *communication*—again."

Miss Pat is always willing to take the time to help educate people on the guidelines regarding guide dogs, but this time she is relieved she can relax from the stressful drive and get some rest. She sits down on the side of the bed with a big sigh. "Whew, it is good to be out of the car and that bad weather." She is caressing my head and running her hand down my back. Yes, that feels good. I lean against her leg and put my head on her knee to let her know I love her too. I hear her tummy rumbling. She must be hungry. Hey, I thought no one was hungry except me!

It is well past the time I am fed. Usually, I eat my supper around four thirty in the afternoon, but because of the bad weather, we had no opportunity to stop. It is now almost 6:30 p.m.—two hours past my dinnertime, and I am hungry! Miss Pat knows I'm hungry as she unzips my little red travel bag and takes out my dog food. Umm, it smells good! That's my food all right! Miss Pat always brings my clean bowl. She puts one and a half cups of my favorite food in the bowl. "Smart Bart sit," she says. I know I am supposed to sit before eating, but she always tells me anyway. I sit very tall and straight until she says, "O.K. good boy," as she gives me permission to eat. I enjoy every morsel to the very last one. Yum-yum, my tummy feels better already! After I finish with my food, she washes my bowl with soap and water and dries it with a paper towel. It is all ready for tomorrow morning.

8

Miss Pat tells Pop we will be right back. We are going out so I can have a potty break. The rain has stopped. Back on with the harness. Work first: find the grass. Down the walkway we go, her hand firmly holding the harness handle. She says, "Find the grass." I look all around for the grass. There it is—over this way, Miss Pat. She quickly removes my harness. She tells me to, "take a break." This means I can go "busy." Whew, what a relief! That feels better. We need to go back now. Pop and Miss Pat have not had dinner. I didn't see a stove in our room, how will she cook supper tonight?

Let's see now, I must remember which room is ours...oh yes, I know, just two more doors down this walkway. Yes, there is Pop. He has the door open. He has been watching out the window for us.

I was right: no stove in this room. No cooking tonight. Pop says we will eat in the restaurant. Of course, he did not mean I would be eating there. I don't eat people food, remember. I always go with Miss Pat because she depends on me. Miss Pat and Pop are freshening up so they can go to the restaurant dining room.

Before we go out again, she has to put my harness back on for me. She always removes my harness for my personal time. That is because during these times, I am "off duty" as she calls it. Pop, Miss Pat, and I walk down the covered walkway to the dining room. She seems happy and relieved that the storm seems to be almost over. Pop walks along side, as they talk about the rest of our trip.

Pop is saying that maybe we should leave very early in the morning to make up for lost time. Miss Pat agrees that is a good idea. I spot the door to the restaurant just about the time she says, "find the door Smart Bart!" I stop as we approach the door, and Pop holds the door open for us to enter the dining room.

There are many people are in the dining room. It is warm and the restaurant smells good! I smell cheeseburgers, corn, and apple pie, all of Pop's favorites! That is "people food," so I know it is not for me. The greeter instructs us to follow her. She has a nice table ready. We follow her to a table in the corner, which has plenty of room underneath the table for me. Miss Pat gives me a quiet command and says, "Down under, Bart." I lay quietly under the table as they look over the menu.

The tablecloth is hanging down from the table. I peer out from underneath it. Here come some feet approaching our table. I sure hope they do not tell us again that I am not to be here! Two big feet with brown loafers, two little feet with blue and white sneakers—one man, one little boy!

"You sure have a well behaved dog there," the man with the big feet said. "Yes, thank you," replies Miss Pat. "May we pet him," asks the man. "I appreciate you asking, but he is working and he should not be petted while he is on duty, because it may distract him. I do appreciate you wanting to pet him, he is a wonderful guide dog," she tells the tall man. She leans nearer to the small child and tells the boy "This is Smart Bart, he is a Labrador and he loves children. He has a special job to do because he is a guide dog."

The little boy seems to understand I am not the family pet, as he peeps under the tablecloth to get a better look. He stoops down, squats on one knee, and stares me right in the face. We are looking at each other—eye-to-eye, nose-to-nose. The boy has big brown eyes and so do I. He wrinkles his nose and I wrinkle mine back. He giggles. The boy smells like french fries and catsup. Yep, that's catsup on his face all right! I am tempted to lick it off, but I was trained never to do things like that. Besides, that would not be polite.

I hear the tall man asking where I was trained. He smiles down at me. I blink to let him know I see his smile. Miss Pat does not mind when she is asked about where I was trained, because it gives her a chance to tell them about Southeastern Guide Dogs and the well-trained dogs there. The man chats with Pop and Miss Pat until the food arrives. The small boy is still under the table with me. He rubs my head and kisses my nose. The tall man and the small boy are now leaving, knowing more about guide dogs.

The boy looks back, waving to me. I sure wish I could play, but I cannot, not tonight. Maybe I will see them again tomorrow when I am not in harness. No, I don't think so, I remember Pop said we would be leaving very early—before daylight. I hope the boy understands that I would have liked to play, but my job must always come first.

9

The rain stopped sometime during the night, the air now smells so clean and fresh. I have had my breakfast and Miss Pat has me settle down in the back seat of our car. It is a great beginning to this day and we all feel rested and refreshed. I heard Pop say we only have about five more hours of driving. I will take a nap until the next rest area. After awhile, I hear Pop say, "we have just passed the 'Welcome to North Carolina' sign." That means we still have a few more hours to ride, but we will be in the mountains soon! He tells Miss Pat that we will be there well before dark.

Our stay will be in a rented cottage. I hope it is as nice as the picture we saw on the Internet web site. We are lucky to have friends with their own houses on the mountain. They often invite us to stay with them, but not on this trip, they all have other guests.

Many folks from Florida go to visit their family and friends in the mountains in the summer, but it is my first time. It is hot in the summertime where we live. I have heard it is always cool on top of the mountain. Some Florida people go north in summer, some people living in the north come south to Florida in the winter! Go figure—people really do the strangest things

We will be happy to see our friends from Florida again. Mr. Cecil and Miss Bonnie left several months earlier to go to the North Carolina Mountains. In Florida, they grow good juicy oranges so they have time to go to their mountain house until the oranges ripen and are ready for picking in the fall. Then it will be time to travel back home.

The orange trees bloom in early spring. The tiny white blossoms are very fragrant. They fill the air with a sweet smell. Mr. Cecil has many people back home to help him with the groves. He has family nearby who also have orange groves. His sister is Miss Vera Jo and her husband is Mr. Buck. They have much to do to prepare the soil and add the *nutrients*. This will help the trees produce strong blossoms which later turn into sweet tasting fruit.

Mr. Cecil and Miss Bonnie built a log house near the National Forest in the mountains of North Carolina. Their house is up on English Ridge Road. They only live in their log house in the summer. During the winter, they live in Florida. Mr. Cecil manages his orange groves, Miss Bonnie volunteers at the animal shelter and the guide dog school where I was trained. She has many animals at home. Miss Bonnie loves animals especially dogs. Bonnie and Mr. Cecil became a host family for a breeder dog that belongs to the guide dog school.

I was born at Miss Bonnie's house in Florida. Miss Bonnie took care of my mama. My mama's name was Pixie and she was so beautiful. She was also a Labrador with soft blonde hair and big bright eyes like mine. She came from the guide dog school to live with Miss Bonnie as a mama dog breeder. I would eventually grow up and go to that same school, but I was to learn how to become a guide dog.

Mr. Cecil and Miss Bonnie are like our family. First, they were my family, but now they are Miss Pat and Pop's family too. Miss

Bonnie met my master, Miss Pat, when Miss Pat was a student at the guide dog school.

Miss Bonnie told her all about Pixie, my mama, and about my birth. They became friends that day. Later that night, Miss Pat called Pop on the phone and said, "I have met someone very special today. I will know her and love her for the rest of my life." She was talking, of course, about Miss Bonnie.

10

When I was born, I was not much bigger than your hand. Everyone was eager to see the new puppies and me, but Miss Bonnie told them they would need to wait until we were bigger and stronger. She was afraid that someone might sneeze on us or spread germs that might make us sick.

Miss Bonnie took us to the *veterinarian* soon after we were born. This is how I met my friend in the white coat, Dr. Paul. Dr. Paul is a very tall man, with a gentle smile and tender heart. He has an office with lots of shiny silver tables and counters full of funny stuff like glass containers full of cotton balls, Q-tips, a light to peek into my ears, and something else that he uses to listen to my heart. Dr. Paul listened to my heart and tummy the day I was born. I was a strong little pup. After checking over the entire litter of my brothers, sisters and me, Dr. Paul said that all of us were very healthy. He told Miss Bonnie that we needed good nourishment from mama Pixie, vitamins, clean water, exercise, and lots of love.

He also told her we would need our puppy shots in a few weeks. At that time, I did not know what that meant. I do now! When that day came for me to get my puppy shots, he was very gentle and assured me it would keep me strong and healthy. As Dr. Paul gave me the injection, he held me close. His white coat smelled clean, like laundry soap.

Mama Pixie was also fine after giving birth and was glad to learn her puppies were all healthy. She had so much to do to take care of us besides just feeding us. She never complained about the extra work and was very gentle with us. Mama took excellent care of us. She washed behind our ears, snuggled with us, and made us behave when we got too rowdy. If we misbehaved, or got too far away from her, mama would pick us up by the back of the neck and give us a little shake. This is what I learned is called a *litter* correction. It doesn't hurt, but it sure got my attention! I often got into trouble when I was a little pup, but as I got bigger, I learned to settle down and behave.

Mama helped me grow strong and confident. She was a wonderful mama. Mama died when I was seven years old. This made us all very sad, especially Miss Bonnie. Miss Bonnie and Miss Pat both think that I will see her again someday. She will be waiting to greet me on the other side of the rainbow in the sky, the entrance to the "Meadow of Fun."

The "Meadow of Fun" is a place I have imagined where all our pet friends go to live after they have passed away from this earth. All the animals are happy there and full of life. They are jumping, running, and having a great time in the meadow that is made just for them. There is plenty of fresh water and lots of food for each special animal. There is even food for the monkeys and the manatees.

At the entrance to the meadow is a huge *rainbow*! It is brilliant with colors of red, blue, purple, green, orange, and yellow. I call it the "Rainbow of Hope."

I think of the meadow as being lush and green with lots of places to run and hide. There are rocks to jump up on, bubbling streams to play in, cool lakes and lily ponds and beautiful butterflies everywhere! Many animals have gone on to live there such as cats and kittens, birds and bats, chickens and ducks! There are also pot-belly pigs, rhinos, hippos, lions, and lambs. They all get along together and play all day. At night, they rest and lay down beside each other sleeping peacefully. There are so many animals, that it's hard for me to imagine them all. What other animals do you think may be there?

Someday I believe I will see my friends that have passed away and gone ahead to the meadow. I have a special friend there already. His name is Nikki. He is a Siberian husky with bright blue eyes, and gray and white fur. Nikki was my first and very best dog friend. I wonder if Nikki has met my mama Pixie.

I think God watches over the meadow. He provides for all the needs of the animals. You see God loves them too, just as we loved them on this earth. I think I will see mama Pixie there someday. I think she will be proud of me and the special work that I do.

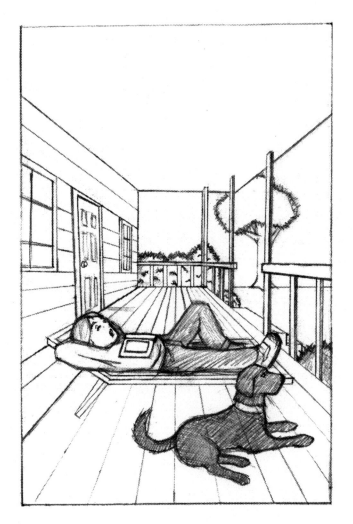

11

We finally arrive at the mountain cottage. Time to unload the car and get settled in. We help Pop bring our stuff into the cottage. We need to be sure to place everything where Miss Pat can find it later. Pop tells her where he places everything and she will remember where they are located.

We take a tour through the entire house. It is a very nice cottage. It smells fresh and clean. Lots of room and very comfy beds. Miss Pat has brought my special comforter from home for my bed. I will sleep on the floor next to her side of the bed in case she needs me. Pop opens the windows to let in the fresh mountain air. We then all walk out onto the wooden deck.

The deck is large, with a very sturdy railing and a good strong gate. "There are four big rocking chairs out here," Pop says, "all facing a breathtaking view." Yes, we will enjoy our stay here. As they both sit down in the chairs, I laid down beside Miss Pat. I listen as they discuss all the things we would see and do on our first summer vacation together. Pop tells us, "later, we will take a short walk all around the outside of the cottage to make sure it is safe for everyone."

Pop wants to relax from the long drive. He has a good book he wants to read. He pulls up one of the big rocking chairs on the deck near the railing, where he can prop his feet up. Several minutes later, he is sleeping and the open book falls softly to the deck floor. Miss Pat smiles as she covers him with an afghan she got from the house. "He must be very tired," she says quietly. She murmurs with a sigh, "I wish I could help him with all the driving."

The sun is warm on our faces, but the air is very cool! The trees are whispering to us as the breeze rustles through the leaves. "They sound like they are whispering and singing." "A song of whispering hope," Miss Pat says. I wonder if she is talking to me or to the trees.

There is so much to see here. Everything to me is new. Just as I turn, I see a *chipmunk*! He is small and brown with some tiny white spots. He stands up on his hind feet, looks around, and then *scurries* across the path leading into the woods as if he is not afraid at all. I wonder if he lives nearby. Maybe he would like to be my friend while we are here.

Many of my friends are people friends, but I especially like my animal friends. That is why I am so excited about being here. Miss Bonnie has brought many of my doggy friends from Florida with her to the mountain. I cannot wait to see them, but work comes first.

After the long drive, I am ready to go for a walk. It will be several more hours before dark. We would have time to go for a walk if we leave soon. Miss Pat must be thinking the same thing because she calls out, "Come, Smart Bart, we will take a short walk." I run to find my leash and my harness where she had put them by the door when we first came in. She will get them for me, but first, she puts on her hiking boots. She grabs the backpack from the chair. She gently wakes Pop to tell him we will be back soon, and we will stay on the nature trail. She gives him a kiss on the cheek as he mumbles, "O.K., hurry back and please be careful." Then she turns and walks back into the cottage. Hey, wait a minute; I thought we were going for a hike! Oops, I need my harness, and it's still inside. She never forgets.

I am eager to go. What is taking Miss Pat so long in the cottage? I push on the screen door; she hears me and comes to let me in. She says, "Come Smart Bart, follow me." As I follow her to the kitchen, I watch closely as she gets the things we will need for the afternoon.

She prepares a backpack for both of us carefully placing a granola bar, graham crackers, and an apple inside. It all looks good, especially the apple. I begin to worry—where is my food? Just about the time I think she is going to zip up the backpack, she fills a little plastic baggie with several cups of my favorite dry dog food and an extra apple. Umm good, that one is for me. She then gets our new canteen, washes it carefully, and fills it with cold water. She says we will share. I like it when she says, "Smart Bart, we can share this." I know that God wants us to share what we have with others and with animals. We talk about this quite often. Actually, she talks and I listen.

The backpack seems ready. She looks for my harness. Yes, here it is on the hook by the door right where she left it. She puts my harness over my head and fastens it *securely*. As she puts on her backpack, she picks up a shiny whistle and the cellular phone that is on the counter. We always take them with us when Pop is not with us. She drops both of them in the side pocket and pulls the zipper up tight.

We return to the deck to tell Pop we are leaving. He is beginning to wake up from his short nap. "See you later," she calls over her shoulder. We cross the deck; I lead her to the gate. She opens the gate and carefully proceeds. I stop before the first step. She tells me, "good boy" as we continue down the steps. One, two, three—only three steps to the ground. She used to have to count steps before she had me. I let her know when we get to the stairs by stopping at the top. I also stop at the bottom landing so she knows where the level ground is. I learned this in my school.

She gives the command "find the path." That was a command she taught to me after my training. I learned that from her a long time ago as we went on walks with the grandchildren: Andrew, Jennifer, Katie, and Madalyn Ruth. When they come to visit, they occasionally go for walks with us.

Carefully I lead her to the path into the woods. It is wide enough for us to walk side by side comfortably. I am always on her left side. She holds the harness handle firmly in her left hand.

I wonder if I will see the little chipmunk again on the path. If he doesn't already have a name, I think I will call him "Charlie." Yes, that will be his name, "Chipmunk Charlie." As we follow the path, I do not see Charlie, but that is O.K. I cannot play right now anyway, because when I am wearing my harness I am on duty.

Wow! I'm beginning to get tired already. It is very hard to breathe this high up on the mountain. Could I be out of shape? We exercise everyday, so I should be in great shape. Miss Pat is breathing hard as well. She is slowing down. We have only been walking about fifteen minutes so I wonder why we are getting so tired. At home, we can walk for hours without feeling this tired. Maybe it is because the path has become steeper as we go up higher on the mountain. Finally, Miss Pat says, "Smart Bart, let's take a break."

That means we can stop and she will take off my harness. Good, I'm ready!

"Here's a nice clearing, we can rest here." The clearing has a big flat rock that looks like a bench. This is truly a beautiful spot. The sun is shining through the trees and there are many wildflowers all around the clearing—blue, pink, white, and yellow. She takes off the backpack and puts it on the rock, careful not to hit the pocket holding the cell phone. As she took off my harness she said, "Smart Bart, take a break—would you like to have a snack with me?" "Yes, yes, I would," I want to say as my tail wags vigorously in response. She laughs as she starts taking a few treats from the backpack.

She takes out an apple first, then some graham crackers. She takes a bite out of the apple, but does not eat it. Instead, she puts the small bite in her hand and says, "Here Smart Bart, this is for you." Then, she takes a big bite out of the apple for herself.

As we finish our snack, we rest on the warm rock and I think about our day. I stretch out in the sweet smelling grass near the rock where she is sitting, but I stay close to her feet. I will not go away from her. Even when the harness is off, I always stay close by just in case she needs me.

Miss Pat reaches down to caress my head, and she tells me what a good dog I have been all day. Yes, exploring on our own is fun. There will be many more days of hiking with our friends, walking the trails and experiencing new things. But today, it is just Miss Pat and I enjoying our special time together.

12

Melodie   *Brummen*

The clouds are dancing across the North Carolina blue sky. It is a long and lazy summer afternoon. She begins to <u>hum</u> one of my favorite <u>tunes</u>. She often does this when we having our quiet time together. I look up to see her, but her face is not looking back at me. Her chin is tilted upward toward the clouds. She is humming to God I think.

Suddenly she stops humming and says, "This dry air sure makes me thirsty. Are you thirsty too, Smart Bart?" She opens the canteen and pours water in a small bowl for me. "Not too much at first" she says, as I take in a big drink. She is thirsty too. She takes a long drink for herself from the canteen. The late afternoon air is warm and I can smell the damp moss on the north side of the rock.

I know we will not be staying at the rock very much longer. It is getting much cooler now as the clouds are beginning to darken and cover the sun. I remember her telling Pop we would be back before dark. I stand and stretch; we must enjoy these last few minutes, and then back to the cottage. We are tired. It has been a long day.

Pop knows I will guide us back safely, but he is always happy and relieved when we get back from one of our walks. Today especially, he will be waiting. This is all very new to me and I must be very careful as I have much to learn about mountain trails. As we head back, I hear Miss Pat talking to someone but she is not talking to me. She is talking quietly to God—thanking God for the lovely time of refreshing and for His love and protection.

As we head back, walking seems much easier traveling down the trail. I finally see the last bend in the trail! I see it Miss Pat! Yes, it's the cottage. There is Pop standing on the deck waving to us. He calls out, "Bart, good boy! I was hoping you and Mom would be back soon."

Pop greets us both with a big hug and says he has started our dinner. It is getting too cool to eat outside but he has made a small fire in the fireplace. Just imagine, it is late July and it is so cool outside that we need a fire to warm us. Well, that is the way it is in the mountains. The weather changes very quickly. As we enter the cottage, I hear the crackling of the small fire and smell the ham warming in the oven. Miss Pat takes off my harness, then unties and removes her hiking boots. She carefully puts both away near the door so that they are ready for tomorrow.

Miss Pat finishes setting the table as Pop pours them both a glass of milk. The warm bread, cheese, and baked ham will taste good to her tonight after the hike up the trail today. She was happy Pop thought about putting the ham in the oven.

As they sit down at the table, Pop takes her hand in his, and then they bow their heads as Pop gives thanks for their many *blessings*. He thanks God for the food, the safe trip, and especially for watching over Miss Pat and me as we were on our afternoon exploration trip on the mountain trail. He ends the prayer with a quiet "amen."

They looked tired, but content. I am tired too. I am trying not to fall asleep, because I have not had my supper yet. Miss Pat will feed me after she has had her dinner. Then I will snooze by the warm fire. They are enjoying their time together here at the cottage already. It is good to be on our first summer vacation together.

13

Miss Pat's friends have phoned this morning welcoming us to the mountain. Miss Bonnie, Lois-Lynn, Sally, and Alice. They did not have the long drive yesterday. They have been here several months already, since early spring.

After a good night's rest and hearty breakfast for all, I hear Miss Pat tell Pop we are going on a real long hike today with her friends. It is Wednesday. Pop says he will be playing golf with the men today. Every Wednesday he says they play something called a "scramble." I don't think it has anything to do with eggs. What do you think? It is probably just the name of their golf game.

He is glad to get to play golf with the men. Pop has not seen Mr. Cecil since May and it is now mid-July. They will have a good time today. The weather is perfect. "It will be difficult on this golf course because of the big hills and many woods," Pop says. Not like home, where the golf course is mostly flat. He calls this course a "challenge." There are many trees, ponds, even a wooden bridge over the cold mountain stream.

They will ride in a golf cart instead of walking because of all the big hills. It would be much too tiring to carry the golf bags on their shoulders. Pop tells us he will have lunch at the club and they will probably be back around four o'clock this afternoon. Miss Pat says that's fine, it will give the girls plenty of time on Big Bald Mountain to pick blueberries and walk the trails.

I have heard it is called Big Bald Mountain because there are no trees that grow on the very top. It is just a flat smooth rock so it looks bald. It is a very long hike, over a mile. Sometimes they go in the red jeep or in the green pick up truck. I heard Lois-Lynn say sometimes, when the weather has not been bad, they can drive all the way to the top of Big Bald. Other times, they can only drive so far and then they have to hike the rest of the way up. Since there was a big storm a few days ago, we can only drive part of the way and will need to hike the rest of the way up to the top.

I know how to hike the trail after our short excursion yesterday. However, I do remember feeling out of breath and Miss Pat had trouble breathing too. I keep hearing about high *altitude*—whatever that is. I wonder if that is what made me so tired as we walked yesterday. Pop said last night, "high altitude means the air is thin and contains less oxygen. The higher up we go, the thinner the air, the more difficult it is to breath. After a few days, our lungs will adjust and it will be easier to breathe as we walk the mountain."

Today is also a perfect day to pick blueberries. We load up the pickup truck with buckets to hold the wild berries. Miss Pat's friends have all arrived and they are bubbling over with excitement. Everyone talks at one time. How do they know who said what? The deck of the cottage is now full of ladies in shorts and hiking boots; one, two, three, plus Miss Pat. I will be the only "boy" going with the women today. The chill from the previous night is now gone and the sun is shining brightly.

They put their jackets on the back seat. It will be much cooler at the top of "Old Bald." Wow, four girls, four jackets, two buckets, water bottles, and a dog! Lois-Lynn starts the engine and we're off! The pickup truck bounces and bangs on the rough road going up. Miss Pat is holding onto me tightly so I do not fall out. Ouch, that last bump hurt. The old road has many deep ruts from previous rains; it is getting too bad for the truck to go much further. Lois-Lynn says, "O.K., that's about as far as the truck will go up the mountain." She stops the truck then tells everyone to get their jackets and the water. She reminds us not to forget the buckets.

Miss Pat moves closer to the tailgate of the truck and swings her legs over the side. Still sitting, she holds out my harness and asks Sally to hold it until she can get down. Sally gladly assists and takes my harness in her hand. Looking at me Sally says, "It's O.K. Bart, jump down." Nope! I will not move until Miss Pat says it is O.K. Miss Bonnie tells Miss Pat it is safe for her to step onto the ground from the pickup truck. I cannot help her at this point, I stay put as I am told, and she will let me know when she needs me. Be careful, there, she is down. She extends my leash as long as it will go and this gives me ample room to jump off the back of the truck. "Come, Smart Bart." This is a familiar command from my master. There, now I'm down. She puts my harness back on and this makes me feel much more confident. I am ready now to help her whenever she needs me.

Sally asks, "Is there anything I can do to help?" "No thanks, I'm fine. Just tell me if there are any holes or big rocks on the ground near my feet," said Miss Pat. "No, you are all clear," Sally said. Miss Pat appreciates her friend's offer to help if needed, but at the same time, her friend allows her to do as much as she can by herself.

14

It was hard for Miss Pat to accept help when she first lost her eyesight. She is very independent. Since we became a team, I have heard her say that she is so blessed to have good friends. When things seen too difficult to handle, God puts people in our lives who have a special gift to encourage others. She has often told me this. Miss Bonnie must have that *spiritual* gift of encouragement that Miss Pat talks about so often.

I have heard Miss Pat say, "God wants us to love one another, as He loved us." That must be very hard to do sometimes, because people can really be very "unlovable." Have you ever noticed that your classmates or friends can sometimes be mean and insensitive to your feelings? When we have visited some elementary schools, I have seen some kids who do that to others. Students pushing and shoving, wanting to be first in line, not even thinking about the person standing next to them. This behavior is called *selfish* and it not a polite or an acceptable way to act. You may ask, "How can you love people different from yourself, or students who may say hurtful things. And besides, why should we?"

This special love can be in our hearts "if you know and trust God," says Miss Pat. She often tells the children at Sunday school about two boys in the Bible named Jonathan and David. They made a *covenant* together. That's a promise—a pledge of mutual loyalty and friendship. It is a very interesting story about devotion and friendship. Miss Pat loves her friends, just as Jonathan loved David as his special friend.

Well, I've been day dreaming a bit about friendships, as I watch the girls gather their belongs for the day. It looks like they have everything now. Miss Pat has put the harness on me and has given me a command to "follow." This means I will stay behind the person she has selected for me to follow and walk directly behind them. I have to do this special command when there are no curbs or streets to focus on. It is like travel along a country road without a sidewalk, except today we are walking up a big mountain. Luckily, it is a gradual upward slope.

Lois-Lynn tells the group this is part of the Appalachian Trail. It is a well-worn trail across the mountain range. Many people have walked it in years past. It extends hundreds and hundreds of miles all along the eastern United States. Wow! I must remember this. It will be something I will think about when I hear people talking about this trail.

It is becoming more difficult for me to stay directly behind Miss Bonnie who is in front of me. The grass is tall and gets in my face making it hard for me to see. At this point, the trail is really just a deep rut in the tall grass. I try to peer around Miss Bonnie, but her backpack is in my way. Miss Pat must sense I am slowing down and being more careful. She reassures me, "It's O.K. Smart Bart, you are doing great!" She may think so, but I have my doubts. This is harder than our walk the other night. I guess I was not as prepared as I thought.

Miss Pat tells the girls ahead they can walk their normal pace, and that we will lag a little behind because we are not used to the trail. She says we will stay close enough to hear them. As we lag behind, I can still see Miss Bonnie ahead of us. Their bodies seem to be getting smaller as they get farther ahead, but I can still hear them talking and laughing. They don't seem to have the same trouble with the thin air as we do. However, they have been here all spring and summer so I think their bodies are accustomed to the altitude.

Wait! Stop! There, on the trail! What is it? I must not allow Miss Pat to continue any further! I stop immediately. "Miss Pat, stop!" She does not move.

I stand perfectly still. She knows if I stop, she should stop also. She is saying, "No, Smart Bart, we must not stop here, we need to keep up as best we can." However, I know what is best, I know I should not proceed. I will not move! This is called "intelligent disobedience" and it's one of the most difficult concepts a guide dog must understand. I know what is ahead; she does not. I must do what I think is best for her safety. She seems to finally understand that I am not just tired of walking, that there is something very wrong—and it is just ahead of us!

I hear Miss Bonnie call back, "You two slow pokes better catch up if you plan to help pick blueberries." I don't move a muscle. Miss Pat calls out, "Bonnie, come back. What is the matter with Smart Bart? He does not want me to walk ahead!" I hear Miss Bonnie reply, "Don't move, we're coming. Stay there!" In just a minute she is back standing just a few feet ahead of us. I hear Miss Bonnie say, "I see it—Pat, tell Bart to stay!" It's a snake, and I think it is a poisonous one!

There, across the trail, is a four-foot long snake looking for a warm rock to lie on. Unfortunately, he is right in our path. I know about snakes because they had a "pretend snake" at my guide dog school and the training instructors taught me never, never, ever go near one. I had remembered!

I have to make sure Miss Pat does not get near it, or step on it. Miss Pat says in a concerned voice, "Bonnie, what can we do?" Miss Bonnie tells her to just be very still, do not move, that she is watching the snake. She says quietly, "He is crawling away from the trail, headed for a sunny rock to the left of you—about ten feet away." I'm so glad Miss Bonnie knows instinctively how to give Miss Pat calm and clear verbal directions of where the snake is and in what direction it is moving.

The snake seems completely unaware of the danger he has put us in. I watch as I see it slither off the path, however, I still do not move. Miss Pat is still standing still, almost rigid. Her hand is trembling on the harness and making it shake a little bit. "Don't be afraid" I want to tell her, but I can't. I can only let her know by the confidence in my body that we will be all right.

Miss Bonnie is closer now and says, "I can see it clearly now, it is not a bad snake. It's just a black snake. It will not hurt us." I'm greatly relieved! "He's gone now," she tells us. By now, the other girls, Lois-Lynn, Sally, and Alice, are here to make sure everyone is safe. Miss Bonnie hurries to our side and tells Miss Pat to walk ahead quickly. Miss Pat gives me a firm command, "Bart, forward" meaning I should proceed straight ahead, and by the tone of her voice, this time quickly!

We go only a few more feet up the trail, when Miss Pat gives me another command. "Bart, easy. Bart, sit," she says. I follow her commands exactly, as she bends over to give me a big hug and kisses me on top of my shiny black head. "What a good boy you are! I'm so proud of you," she says excitedly. I can't stop wagging my tail when she is praising me—swish, swish, swish goes my long Labrador tail. She is glad I learned about snakes when I was in guide dog school. Yes, I know my job—and I do my job well! She knows to trust in me when I let her know we need to stop. Just like today, when we needed to stop immediately!

We all begin to relax now that the snake is past. Now that the scare is over, everyone starts to laugh again, saying the men will never believe what we encountered this morning. They are saying they plan to tell Pop how brave I was. I know I was just doing my job. It is not much further to the top of old Big Bald. I really need some water and it will be good to have my harness off for a few minutes. I can sure use a break.

15

We have rested at the top for about fifteen minutes. The water was cool and the girls had a snack that Sally brought to share with everyone. Lois-Lynn says it's time to get the buckets and start picking blueberries for tonight. They plan to have blueberry cobbler as a special treat for dessert! They all scramble to their feet, with buckets in hand. Miss Pat decides she will stay close to the girls just in case we encounter another critter like before.

There are so many blueberry bushes. The bushes are full of berries! The girls pick some—and eat many. I just watch as Miss Pat fills the bucket Sally is holding. I wonder why they seem to enjoy these little berries so much. They gave me one and I did not like it. I prefer a slice of apple with peanut butter, or better yet, my food.

Miss Pat and her friends all look very funny. They laugh at each other, because their mouths have turned blue! The juice from the blueberries has stained not only their mouths, but also their tee shirts and shorts too. As they fill the buckets, they say we will have plenty to make a big blueberry *cobbler* for tonight. Friends are coming over after supper and there will be plenty of cobbler for all to enjoy.

I hear Lois-Lynn say that Miss Dorothy, who lives at the bottom of the mountain, will come tonight. Also, Miss June, Mr. Al, Mr.

Louie, and of course Mr. Cecil. Pop will be there too. We will have to tell them all about the snake. Well, not me—the women will tell the story. I just hope they do not make it a "whopper of a story." After picking the berries, they all sit down to rest before heading back down the mountain.

It is very quiet here. Just nature sounds. On top of Big Bald Mountain, we don't hear the sound of cars, cell phones, radios, or TV's. No city noises, just the wonderful sounds of the birds. Sometimes we can hear the scurrying of little animals, like the baby rabbits. I even saw a raccoon and a deer earlier today.

The breezes make the leaves wiggle and jiggle, creating soothing sounds. I guess this is how the trees talk to each other. We listen to the trees as they talk amongst themselves. It is quiet and no one is talking. We can feel the presence of God and all the wonder of His creation. God made all this beauty for us to enjoy and we should take care of it. In our backpacks, we have trash bags to pick up our snack papers. We will make sure we leave the trail and Big Bald Mountain clean.

Animals on the mountain should not find leftover people food or trash. They eat wild berries, grasses, leaves, beetles, ants, and nuts that have fallen from the trees. God has provided an abundance of food for them. Some of the animals sleep during the day and eat at night when it is quiet and there are no people around. When we eat our dinner tonight, we will ask God to bless our food, and thank Him for His abiding love and *provisions* for us and the animals.

I heard Miss Bonnie say we were going to visit Miss Dorothy again later this afternoon. They want to invite her and her husband over for supper. I remember her! We stopped to meet Miss Dorothy and her husband, Mr. Ernie, on the way up the mountain.

Miss Bonnie had given us their name and address before we left home. Miss Bonnie had said to Miss Pat, "Dorothy knows the mountain like the back of her hand." Mr. Ernie even built the house they live in. It is a beautiful wooden house with a big deck. Their house sits high above he road, perched on the side of the mountain overlooking the pasture. That area is called "Mt. Laurel." It was named after the flowers that grow abundantly all around this area.

Miss Dorothy had been happy to see us, and she loves dogs! We did not get to stay long yesterday, as we were in a hurry to find the cottage. I will be glad to see her and Mr. Ernie again. We have plenty of blueberries to share with them.

I heard the women talking about stopping by Miss Dorothy's garden to gather some vegetables to go with our dinner. They helped Miss Dorothy plant the big garden in the spring. They cannot plant when the ground is frozen from the snow and cold winter, but when the ground is warm, Miss Dorothy will go to the barn and get her tractor to till the garden. Then it will be ready to plant. Many of Miss Dorothy's friends help her plant and weed the garden. It is a big job. They also help with the picking when it is time to harvest the vegetables in midsummer through fall. Do you know what *"harvest"* means?

Miss Dorothy shares the vegetables she grows with Miss Bonnie, Lois-Lynn, Sally, Miss June, Mr. Al, and many others. She always plants extra veggies for the little critters that may creep into the garden at night looking for a healthy midnight snack. Then there are the wonderful black raspberries that grow on the long wooden fence by the winding driveway. She planted the berry bushes many years ago and now they bear much fruit every year.

God provides the sun and the rain to make the garden plentiful. He knows the people in this area need food for winter. God is at work when we do not even realize it.

16

Miss Dorothy brought Miss Pat and me to visit a college in Mars Hill, North Carolina. The road leading down the mountain to Mars Hill was steep and winding. It had signs all along the roadway indicating we should drive with caution because of a *steep* grade. Trucks must drive very carefully since they are big and carry heavy loads. Miss Dorothy is a safe driver and knows the mountain roads extremely well. She said she had driven these roads thousands of times.

The day we went to Mars Hill College, we met some of the people she used to work with. I think they enjoyed meeting us, especially me. They said they had never had a guide dog on campus before. School was out for the summer, so we toured the school and walked around the campus grounds. Later we sat on a bench under a big oak tree. Miss Dorothy told Miss Pat all about the history of the school. It was another day of learning for us.

We made new friends at the college and have made new friends on the mountain. Some were from Florida, some from Texas, and many from North Carolina. Miss Pat wanted to know what they liked to do while they are here. We found out that they liked to go fishing, visit the pottery barn, and see a good play or concert every few weeks. Once a week someone will visit the farmers market in

Asheville to pick up supplies. Next week there is a concert in Mars Hill. Miss Pat loves music, usually good and loud!

Miss Dorothy tells Miss Pat about a good movie playing at the local movie theater today. She says, "Pat would you like to go?" "Yes, we would love it." Of course, I am always included. Remember, I go wherever Miss Pat goes.

Many blind people enjoy movies. Miss Pat does. I'm sure it may seem a bit strange when you are standing in line at the movie theater and you see a blind person with their guide dog, or maybe with their white red-tipped cane. You may wonder, if they can't see the movie, why would they come? I know what Miss Pat would say. She would say, "movies can be fun and entertaining, especially the ones with a great story to tell, and lot of *dialogue.*"

Since being with Miss Pat, I have learned blind people love to have fun and do exciting things as well as sighted people. They just enjoy things a little differently. While Miss Pat can't see the action on the screen, she listens intently to the actors and the story line. Now, sometimes we do have a problem. It is usually when the people sitting behind us are being loud and not *considerate* of the people around them. This makes it difficult for all to enjoy the movie. This does not happen often however, and most people are generally very nice and quiet.

Miss Pat and I go to the movies with Pop most of the time. He takes us places we want to go. I think Pop likes to go to the movies because of the great popcorn! I love popcorn too, but guide dogs are not allowed to eat anything off the floor.

Today we are going to a two-o'clock *matinee.* At the early showing, the floor of the movie theater is usually very clean. No one has spilled soda or popcorn on the floor yet. After we have our tickets,

Miss Pat gives me the command to follow Miss Dorothy. I know what follow means; I learned that while in guide dog school along with the many other commands. However, following in a movie theater is not easy. There are so many people, so many legs, so many feet, all going in various directions. I guess they don't all want to go see the same movie we have chosen.

It gets very dark as we enter the corridor leading to our movie. I am not afraid. I know to stay close behind Miss Dorothy. I have been told to follow. I will do exactly that. Miss Dorothy finds us a good seat. She tells Miss Pat where the nearest exit sign is. I listen carefully. Miss Pat nods her head as she gets a picture of her surroundings in her mind. I lay down quietly at her feet as the movie begins. Wow! That was a loud noise! It's just the start of the movie. I am trained not to be afraid of loud noises. I know there is no danger with this loud noise; it is only part of the movie. Besides, this is a great time for me to take a little snooze. I don't really take an actual nap. I must be ready get up immediately in the event Miss Pat needs to leave her seat, or in the unlikely event of an emergency. Good, everyone seems to be all settled now and enjoying the movie. I am content too. I am so happy that I will be assisting Miss Pat for the rest of my life. I love her and I know that she loves me.

After the movie is over, the sun is shining brightly. We have visited the college and have gone to a movie. It is now late afternoon. Miss Dorothy tells Miss Pat that we can go fishing at the pond when we get back. She loves fishing and so does Miss Pat.

Have you ever gone fishing? I have never been fishing, but our new friends, Miss Dorothy and her husband, Mr. Ernie, get to fish whenever they want. They have their own fishing pond in their cow pasture. When anyone wants to go fishing, all you need to do is call

Miss Dorothy to see if it is O.K. She never says no to the folks on the mountain. She says, "of course, come on down!"

Some ponds are just plain old ponds—this one is very, very special. This fishing pond has a name, it is called "Ernie's Pond." Mr. Ernie built the pond many years ago with Miss Dorothy's help. They liked it so much, that they built a second pond nearby.

They have a big water wheel on the bigger pond which helps pump water into the lower pond. Mr. Ernie built the water wheel. He is so smart; I think he could do almost anything. I take that back, I heard Miss Dorothy say today, "Ernie can do anything he sets his mind to. That is, if he wants to." Mr. Ernie has a strength inside that you can't see from the outside. Miss Pat has told me, she can hear in his voice that he had strength of character. She says that having good character is more important than any other kind of strength. I can tell that she likes Mr. Ernie a lot. He is calming to her. Often she is frustrated because she can't see, and he quietly tells her, "take your time, we are in no hurry." I have noticed Mr. Ernie never gets in a hurry either.

The pond is stocked with rainbow trout, a fish of many colors. Bright and shiny just like a rainbow. Have you ever seen a rainbow? I have. Miss Pat sits on the side of the pond with her fishing rod and her "dough balls" that Miss Dorothy has made for everyone to use as fish bait. There are plenty of fish in Ernie's Pond.

Miss Pat has caught two fish already! The fish must love the dough balls. Pop takes the fish off the hook and puts them on a stringer. He will leave the stringer in the water until Mr. Cecil is ready to clean the fish. Right now Mr. Cecil is busy helping Miss Pat with her rod and reel. She has it all tangled up again. Mr. Cecil is patient. He untangles the line and gets her another dough ball for the hook. There, the bait is on now. She casts the fishing line back into the pond. Plop! Just where she wanted it! Mr. Cecil is the one who knows how to clean our fish. Once the fish have been cleaned and washed, we will eat them later for dinner.

Mr. Cecil is always making jokes. He is good at that. He has had lots of practice. He likes to play practical jokes on his friends. He often plays a joke on Miss Pat—like sneaking up behind her and tapping her shoulder. She turns and thinks no one is there because he has stepped quietly way. She doesn't mind. She knows he is just teasing her. She is happy they treat her as if she was not blind. She likes to feel independent and tries to do all the things she can, like fishing and hiking with her friends. She told me today that this place is very special to her. I hope we will be able to come here again.

I love running around the pond and watch the fish jump as Miss Dorothy comes to feed the fish. Oops! I fell in the pond! What a big splash I made! I got too close to the edge and slipped right in, being a Labrador, I loved it. Miss Pat started laughing and said, "it's O.K.—it's O.K. Bart can swim. He loves the water." I do love the water, and wanted to swim longer, but everyone wanted to catch fish for dinner so I had to get out—and stay out! Everyone caught a few fish today. Everyone except me, that is.

We will have plenty of fish for supper. Miss Bonnie said that we would go to Lois-Lynn and Mr. Louie's house to cook the fish. Miss Dorothy will have some for their dinner as well, but they will stay home tonight. Mr. Ernie is not feeling well today so Miss Dorothy will take care of him, as she always does. She loves Mr. Ernie so much. I can see it when she looks at him with such tenderness in her eyes.

Mr. Ernie enjoyed the fishing today as he sat in the gazebo watching all the activity. He has a sparkle in his eye that never seems to leave. I like to watch him enjoying the fun.

I am so glad I met our new friends Miss Dorothy and Mr. Ernie. They have lived on the mountain for many, many years. Mr. Ernie is a kind and gentle man, and speaks softly, which means we have to listen more closely to what he is saying. He likes to tell funny jokes, too. Maybe that's where Mr. Cecil learned to be a such prankster.

Miss Dorothy laughs as Mr. Ernie teases her. She just says, "Now, Ern, you know that is a big whopper of a tale." Miss Dorothy is a tiny woman, with a big heart and laughing eyes. Her skin is very tan with little freckles that come from working in the garden all summer. She has short brown hair sprinkled with gray. She may be small, but she is strong and a very hard worker.

Miss Dorothy takes care of everything at their home-place. She takes care of the horses, works the garden, cans the vegetables, and makes black raspberry jam for the winter. She has honeybees and collects all the honey. It is the best you will ever taste. She even rides a tractor to mow the grass down by the long, winding driveway. Even though she has a lot to do, there is always time for her to spend with Mr. Ernie. He needs her, like Miss Pat needs me. He has been sick for several years, but you would not know it, because he never complains. She prepares Mr. Ernie's favorite foods for breakfast and supper, always served with biscuits and honey. Later, she finds his sweater and makes sure he is comfortable sitting on their big porch overlooking "Ernie's Pond." Mr. Ernie has that twinkle in his eye again as he looks at her. Mr. Ernie loves his life on the mountain with his family.

Mr. Ernie and Miss Dorothy have a son and a daughter who are grown up now, and live in their own houses on the other side of the mountain. Their daughter is named Miss Tammy. She has a yellow Labrador named Cody. Mr. Randy is their son and he has a dog, too. Randy's dog is named "Mutt." Mutt is always muddy from jumping in the pond and all stinky from rolling around out in the pasture.

Miss Dorothy does not allow Mutt to go inside the house. Only Cody and I are allowed inside. Miss Dorothy keeps her house very clean and tidy. No dirty feet or dirty paws allowed in her house, especially Mutt! Well, it's time for us to leave the pond for today. We must get our fish to Mr. Louie's house for supper.

Mr. Louie will be cooking our fresh fish over hot coals on the grill. I will watch from the opposite side of the porch. I am never allowed to go near an outdoor grill. I learned what "hot" means when I was in guide dog school. I am careful Miss Pat does not get to close to the grill, either. She is safely sitting in the porch swing, listening to all the chatter from the group. When your family or friends "cook out" over a hot grill, remember, dogs and kids should not run or get near the hot grill. I hope you will remember this. I do.

Mr. Louie is my new friend and he is Lois-Lynn's husband. He talks kind-of funny to me. I think I heard Miss Pat say it was his "accent." Mr. Louie is French-Canadian by birth and he still speaks with some of that accent even though he is a full American now. He has lived in this country many years.

They live in a big house that Mr. Louie built. It sits above the golf course fairway that runs along the mountain slope. The house was painted dark green with red shutters and trim. It has a very big deck that goes all around the front of the house. There's lots of room for chairs, a big porch swing, and toys for the grandchildren. There is a sign over the door that says, "Welcome to our Mountain House." Mr. Louie and Lois-Lynn love to have people over to their house to visit.

After supper tonight everyone will be staying for bible study. Lois-Lynn has made the blueberry cobbler and it is in the oven to bake. The house smells yummy. Later tonight, everyone will share the cobbler and enjoy it with a cup of freshly brewed coffee.

Lois-Lynn has a family dog named "Princess." I like playing with Princess, except she loves to chase tennis balls, and I am not allowed to run after tennis balls. When I was a puppy in training to be a guide dog, I was taught not to chase balls, squirrels, or bunnies. My puppy raiser family called it a "*distraction.*" It is important in my job not to be distracted when I am working. When I am off duty, we can play chase with each other.

Princess never seems to tire of playing chase, and she does not care what it is she is chasing. She runs down the long narrow steps leading to the golf course, across the fairway, and into the woods, looking for anything to play with. Mr. Louie stands on the deck yelling, "Princess, Princess, come here! Come home, now!" Once she got lost, and everyone had to walk the whole mountain to find her. They don't want that to happen again. I love running around on the big deck while they call for Princess, ducking under the porch swing as Miss Pat throws my toy across the deck. She doesn't throw it hard. This way I don't have to go too far away from her. I may not be on duty right now, but I still want to be close to her in case she needs me.

Here comes Pop! He walks over to sit with Miss Pat. She tells me I can take a "break." This means she feels safe and I can go play. Pop gets up to open the gate on the deck and tells me, "Go play, Bart. But stay in the yard." I understand what that means. I take off running! I run up and down the hill by their big green house. I must remember to stay out of the flowerbeds. Lois-Lynn loves her flowers and does not allow dogs, even me, in her flower garden. She says it is really "God's Garden." She just takes care of it by shooing us out.

She has a small stone angel statue in her garden. Her flower garden is where she sits sometimes as she thinks about their grandchildren. Lois-Lynn wants her grandchildren to know God loves them. She talks to them often about how much God loves them. She prays while she is working in the garden.

Princess and I have been running around the walkways and steps, darting in and around the tall trees. What is that? I hear Miss Pat calling my name. It is time for me to quickly go to her. This is called *obedience*. Princess is slowly sniffing the edge of the path, as she walks back to the house. She is in no hurry to get back. Eventually, she will come. When your mom or dad calls for you, do you come quickly?

17

Today is the big *Silent Auction*. It is a charity event to help raise money for the Madison County *Hospice*. The action is to be held in a big red barn at the bottom of the mountain. Everyone will bring an item that will be donated for this *charity*. Some will bring home-made baked goodies such as muffins, cinnamon raisin bread, banana nut bread, homemade jam and jelly, cakes, and cookies. These items will sell very fast. I guess Miss Pat will buy something for breakfast tomorrow. Her favorite is banana nut bread.

Lois-Lynn is already here. She is busy setting up for all the children's events. There will be much for them to do; games, face painting, apple bobbing, and sack races. Later, there will even be a contest for best costume.

Lois-Lynn is really a clown, but looks like a person most of the time. Her clown name is "Sonshine." She chose that name because she likes to tell children about how much God loves them. God's only Son, Jesus, especially loves the children.

Pop calls her Sonshine all the time, so that's why I think she is a real clown—just in a person body. Today she has painted her face with white paint, big round rosy cheeks, and a red painted on grin that goes from ear to ear. She is truly a very joy-filled clown!

Sonshine's clown suit is very colorful, but much too big for her! She has on big baggy purple and white striped pants, floppy green *thronen* (handwritten)

wackeln (handwritten)
Pom pon (handwritten)

shiny shoes that turn up at the ends. Perched atop her head she has a blue straw hat with a bunch of yellow sunflowers sticking out the top, which jiggles and bobbles as she walks. She is always singing! She likes what she calls "praise and worship songs." God loves to hear His children singing. She is also one of God's children, even if she is a grownup.

Sonshine takes her tape player and places it on the rock ledge near the red auction barn. She puts in a tape, and turns the sound up full blast! The children are all singing along. They seem to know every song. They may not be in tune with the music, or singing beautifully, but it is loud! Miss Pat says God did not say it had to be beautiful, He just said make a "Joyful Noise." Well, I guess that is what they are doing all right!

People are bringing in items for the auction while Sonshine entertains the children. There are balloons filled with helium. Do you know what *helium* is? The helium makes her voice sound like my new friend, Charlie Chipmunk! Speaking of Charlie, I wonder where he is today. Maybe he is hiding. He is missing all the fun, but maybe he is shy. That's O.K., I will tell him all about the auction when I see him. After all, he is my new little critter friend.

There is a lot to do to get ready for the auction today. Some of the things people are bringing to sell are antique clocks, bone china dishes, rare books, hand-painted artwork, owl boxes, a handcrafted

Wind= spiel (handwritten)

wooden porch swing, and wind chimes. So many things! They should make a lot of money to help Hospice.

Something smells good! It's coming from over there, the big tent, near the parking area. Miss Pat has given me a command of "forward." I think she wants to find out what is being served for lunch. The smell gets even stronger as we approach the red and white tent.

The table is loaded with good things to eat as the people line up to buy their favorites. "Cotton candy, warm caramel apples, popcorn hot from the popping machine, hamburgers, hot dogs, pizza, and homemade brownies," the man behind the table yells. Miss Pat would like a more healthy lunch. She asks a lady volunteer if they have any salads, or maybe pasta. "Why, yes," the cheerful volunteer says. "Right over here." She then proceeds to describe the healthier food. She laughs because at an event such as the auction, most people like the other food items the best so that is what sells the most. After saying hello to all the *volunteer* workers, we head back to the red barn, since we told Pop we would be back by twelve o'clock. I just heard Miss Pat's talking watch say, "eleven-forty five a.m." Have you ever seen a watch that talks? All Miss Pat does is push a little button on the side of her watch and it tells her the correct time of day or night. I think that is so cool, don't you?

All the auction items have now been sold, except for the big tub of old golf balls Mr. Louie brought. Nobody wants to buy them. He found them in the woods near the golf course by his house. He doesn't care that they were not sold, he is glad to take them back home. He drags the bag of old golf balls back to his Jeep.

Sonshine is still wearing her wide painted-on grin, but she is tired from all the kids' activities. Her sunflowers are drooping and wilted now. She is packing all the things she brought for her clown act, as Miss Pat helps her with putting stuff back in the boxes. Sonshine says, "Let's see, do I have everything now?" as she looks under the table and around the cartons. "I think that's it," she says. We have the tape player, our tapes, the face paint, the flowers, the stickers, the helium tank, and the leftover balloons. "Nothing left to do but pick up all the balloons that have burst and the trash that has blown over here" she says. Lois-Lynn, Oops—I mean Sonshine, goes about picking up the trash and puts it all in the trashcan that was provided by the volunteers.

Everyone is leaving the barn where the auction was held. The men have put away the tables, swept the old oak floors, put away the brooms, and locked all the doors. They are all excited because the auction was a big success. The money raised will greatly benefit the Hospice of Madison County. I heard Mr. Louie say, "Yes, gentlemen, we need to do this again next year."

The food is all gone. Did Miss Pat get the banana bread? Yes, she did. Good! Miss Pat also bought black raspberry jam and fresh honey made by Miss Dorothy. It will be a good breakfast for Pop in the morning. We head back to our car, walking much slower now because we are so very tired.

We are also dirty from putting everything away in the auction barn. Pop says he is ready for a long hot shower. He looks tired too. He says, "It has been a good day for the Madison County Hospice."

Sonshine waves good-bye as she trips on her big floppy shoes. When she gets home, it will take her a long time in the shower to get all that clown paint off her face. I heard her tell the kids as we left, she will take it off with cold cream. I wonder why she would use it cold—why wouldn't she use warm cream?

Remember, I told you Sonshine's husband, Mr. Louie was a good cook. He is making stew tomorrow and has invited us over after church. We will go. I wonder what is in the stew. I'm sure there are lots of veggies from Miss Dorothy's garden. Sonshine will help with Sunday dinner, but she prefers to sing, play, and pray. Not cook!

Princess, their dog, likes me coming over for a visit, she knows when I have my harness off I love to run and play with her. I am allowed in her house because I am clean and mind my *manners*. Dachboden

Inside the house, Princess runs up and down the stairs to the loft. She likes to hide there. From the bottom of the stairs, I see stacks of papers and books where Lois-Lynn does her office work. She has her computer in the loft too. I sure hope Princess doesn't knock anything over while she is up there. She will get in trouble if she does. I never go up in the loft. I stay downstairs and just watch. The stairs are too narrow for me. Princess is small and I am much bigger. Besides, I am a guide dog, so I have to remember not to take risks when I play. I would not want to injure myself because I need to be strong to help Miss Pat. We only have a few more days left before we have to leave the mountain. It doesn't seem like we have been here for a whole month. Time goes so fast when you are learning new things, meeting new friends, and having fun.

18

We stop by Miss Bonnie and Mr. Cecil's to say goodbye. The road to their house is very bumpy. Pop has to be careful to stay in the middle so that he does not hit one of the big rocks on the gravel road. Miss Bonnie's log-house is on English Ridge Road and it is hard to see from the road because there are so many trees.

"There it is! I see it! Turn here! Turn here, Pop. Easy now, don't go off in the ditch!" That is what I would tell him if I could talk. We are in their driveway now and had no problems with the ditch. As we reach the doorway, we hear a thundering noise coming from the downstairs. "Slow Down!" Bonnie tells the dogs bounding up the stairs. "You guys are going to get hurt."

Bonnie is small and fragile looking, but she is a strong lady. The dogs could run right over her, but with one word from her, the dogs slow down and behave themselves. They heard us coming down the driveway! The dogs know I am here, that's why they are excited! We have been so busy we have had very little time to play at Bonnie's house with all my dog friends. I know what they like to play. It is a game called hide and chase! It is their favorite game. I still have on my harness, my working outfit, so I'm still on "duty." I can't play just yet. I need to make sure Miss Pat doesn't trip on the stone pathway leading up to the log house.

There, I have made sure Miss Pat is safely on the porch. She leans down to unbuckle my harness, takes it off and tells me, "Smart Bart, take a break." I am glad to do just that! I'm coming guys—wait for me!" I can't wait to play with Bonnie's dogs. I wish Cody had been able to come over to play too, but Cody is with Tammy today. They were going to the river to do some rafting with her friends.

Bonnie brought four dogs with her. There's Hank, the English cocker spaniel. He's black and gray in color, and very handsome. I can remember he bit someone one time, right on their behind; I think it was an accident. He does not do that anymore. Then there's Gebra, the red Vizula, she is small, but full of energy. Sundance is the English setter. I especially like Sundance, who was just a puppy when I first met her. I call her Sunny for short.

Look out! Here comes Josie! Josie is only her nickname. It is short for her real name, which is "Josephine." Bonnie calls her Josephine to get her attention when she has disobeyed. Josie is a black, Standard poodle with very curly hair. When we go for our walks, Josie gets to go with us. Miss Bonnie lets Josie wear a sun visor, it has orange and green "gators" printed on it.

Soon, I will have get back in the car to take the long trip back down the mountain and home to Florida. Until then, we will play in the woods behind Miss Bonnie's house. Let's go guys—not much time left!

Miss Pat and Miss Bonnie have a good visit. As they walk down the road I hear them talking about all the things have done together this summer. Miss Pat is alone with Bonnie on the road, she is not afraid. She knows Miss Bonnie will watch out for her. Pop and Mr. Cecil are watching the golf match on T.V. They love golf. I think it sort of a silly game—chasing a little white ball on the green grass. I would rather be chasing the dogs.

As we get ready to leave, Miss Bonnie and Mr. Cecil load Pop and Miss Pat up with fresh tomatoes from the farmers market, as well as honey and homemade raspberry jam from Miss Dorothy. They want us to stay longer. Their other guests have left, and they said we could use the big room upstairs if we will stay another week. Pop explains we have already been gone a month, and he has to get back to work. I will miss everyone. I will especially miss the dogs and Miss Bonnie. For me, it will be a long time to wait to see them again, but I will!

Miss Bonnie and Mr. Cecil will be staying in the mountains until October. They have much to do before they return to their Florida home for the winter. Mr. Cecil wants to finish the new bathroom in their log house basement. He also wants to build a railing to the steps leading upstairs. He said that would be safer for Pop, Miss Pat, and me when we come to visit next year. They will work hard to get their mountain house ready for the long, cold winter. Things will have to be cleaned, put away and covered until next spring. Something will always need to be done around the big log house.

This week they are repairing the fence because Josie keeps jumping over it.

Miss Bonnie will have to help with this by holding the wire while Mr. Cecil pounds the stakes into the moist dirt. Even a higher fence may not keep Josie in. "If she wants out, she will find a way out," says Miss Bonnie. Josie loves to explore the woods and trails and is always in trouble for getting out of the fenced area. She either jumps over it, or digs underneath it. She is a very determined poodle. Once

Josie jumped the fence and Miss Bonnie and Miss Pat drove all over the mountain searching for her. Later that day Josie came walking down the driveway, tired and hungry, and glad to be home. Everyone was glad she found her way home. Josie has a very adventuresome spirit.

I wish we could stay longer. Everything will look so different in the fall. The leaves on the mountain will change colors from the greens of summer, to the brilliant reds, yellows, and rust colors of the fall. The fall season here is particularly beautiful in Eastern North Carolina, maybe even all over the whole state of North Carolina. In nature, everything changes. After the fall leaves change their colors, they will drop off the trees. Winter will put on a spectacular show of glistening ice on the trees and fresh fallen snow on the mountain. I have never seen snow. I hope we can come to the mountain sometime in the winter so I can play in the snow.

It won't be long before it is time to harvest the last of the summer vegetables. Miss Dorothy will dig up all the potatoes, which are left in the garden, and put them in her cool basement for the winter. There may be a few beets left, but the cabbages are all gone. The tomatoes and green beans have all been canned and put away for the winter. Miss Dorothy will make wonderful soups and many tasty suppers this winter from the fall harvest of vegetables.

We won't get to stay for the Harvest Festival this year. The fall festival is held at the little stone church at Mt. Laurel. It is called Bright Hope Church. Miss Dorothy said the proceeds from the Harvest Festival will help raise money for a new roof for the church.

The little church may need a new roof, but its leaded glass windows are beautiful. When the morning sun starts to shine through the glass, bright colors appear on the walls.

The fall festival is famous for homemade Apple Butter made by people from the church. The apples will be ready for picking soon. North Carolina has many apple orchards. The apples are sweet and crisp. I like apples.

The women and some of the men from Bright Hope church will be making the Apple Butter soon. It is a tasty treat of cooked apples, sugar, and cinnamon. Most people like the Apple Butter spooned over a hot, flaky biscuit. They will save some of the apples to make applesauce. They will be put into jars for the long winter.

The festival will be a lot of fun for everyone on the mountain. There will be crafts of all kinds, special singing, hayrides, and a game called, "Horseshoes." Did you know horses let people play with their shoes?

I've had a wonderful summer vacation. For a dog, I've learned many new things that I would not have learned at home. Like the proper way to hike with a blind person—Miss Pat taught me that. I rode in the golf cart down the golf course fairway with Miss Bonnie and Miss Pat. I walked in the pasture without stepping in anything stinky! I went swimming in the pond all by myself—once! Not to mention all the fun I had the day of the charity auction, the craft festival, and oh yes, the concert at Mars Hill College. So many new things we have done, too many for me to count.

Miss Pat and Pop have enjoyed their vacation, too. She has listened to four books on tape, gone for long cool walks with her friends and me. She truly loves the mountain. She looks relaxed and well rested.

Pop enjoyed the mountain golf courses, reading, relaxing from his daily routine, and fishing—even though he did not catch many fish. The trip was just what we all needed this summer. Pop does not seem to mind that he will have a twelve-hour drive back to Florida. I suppose we will stop overnight to get a good night's rest since he is the only one driving. Remember, guide dogs are faithful, dedicated, and smart—but we don't drive!

As we leave the *pristine* beauty of the North Carolina Mountains and head south, I wonder where my next adventure will be. What was that? Did I hear Pop mention a trip out West? "Where is West?" I can hardly wait to go, can you?

The End—of this adventure.

Be sure to follow more of
Smart Bart's adventures.

Glossary

Accommodations—something supplied for convenience or to satisfy a need

Adventure—an exciting or remarkable experience

Aerobics—a system of physically working out or conditioning

Assistance—the act of helping out or supporting

Auction—to sell property to the highest bidder

Awesome-expression of amazement

Blessing—approval or encouragement

Chipmunk—a small striped woodland animal akin to a squirrel

Cobbler—a deep-dish fruit pie with a thick top crust

Command—to exercise a dominating influence over

Communication—an act or instance of transmitting a message

Complicated—difficult to understand

Confidence—faith or belief that one will act in a right, proper, or effective way

Correction—the action or instance of amending

Covenant—a usual formal, solemn and binding agreement

Distracting—to turn aside, divert

Faithful—steadfast in affection or allegiance, loyal

Fellowship—companionship, company

Gulf—a part of an ocean or sea extending into the land

Harness—gear or equipment

Harvest—the season for gathering in agricultural crops

Hospice—a facility or program designed to provide a caring environment for supplying the physical and emotional needs of the terminally ill

Identification—an act of identifying

Impaired—to damage or make worse by or as if by diminishing in some material

Impossible—incapable of being or occurring

Labrador retriever; a dog—a compact, strongly built retriever

Lanai—porch, veranda

Litter—set of offspring at one birth of an animal

Manners—kind

Matinee—a musical or dramatic performance or social or public event held in the daytime and especially the afternoon

Nutrients—nourishment

Policy—government, regulation

Portico—a colonnade or covered ambulatory

Pristine—fresh and clean

Provisions—to supply with provisions

Rainbow—an arc or circle that exhibits in concentric bands the colors of the spectrum

Respect—the act of giving particular attention

Scurries—to move in or as if in a brisk rapidly alternating step

Securely—assured, certain

Solution—an action o process of solving a problem

Spiritual—relating to, consisting of, or affecting the spirit

Transportation—an act, process, or instance of carrying or of being moved

Universe—the whole body of things

Volunteer—one who enters into, or offers himself for a service of his own free will

About the Author

Pat and her husband Cliff live in Florida where she is a member of Southeastern Guide Dogs' Board of Directors. Pat is a highly sought after Inspirational Speaker in the Southeastern United States. With the assistance of her black Labrador, Bart, she is able to lead a successful and rewarding life giving encouragement and hope to others.

Before losing her eyesight, Pat's previous life was her career, which spanned some 20 years in the computer industry. She was a compulsive workaholic, often going days without sleep. She put her health, her family and her faith on hold for the glamour and excitement of the corporate world.

During that time, she received numerous awards for her leadership style and corporate achievements. In 1990, she was recognized in the *Who's Who of National Business Leaders*, but even this did not fill the hole she felt in her heart. However, there came a time when God lead her to new priorities in her life. It started a journey for her that she calls her "Journey of Faith." Pat is currently writing a series of children's Christian books.

In each chapter of this book, there is a little "lesson of life" that she has learned through her own walk of faith. Pat shares a few of these lessons with you. Since losing her eyesight, she now "walks by faith, not by sight" and she now sees more with her heart than she has ever seen with her eyes.

978-0-595-33410-0
0-595-33410-5